Zoobooks®

Hippos

The hippopotamus is, without a doubt, one of the strangest-looking animals in the world. The ancient Greeks named this large, lumbering animal "hippopotamus," which means "river horse." But hippos are not related to horses.

Found only in Africa, hippos come in two varieties. The small *pygmy hippo* lives in rain forests and swamps. And the gigantic *common hippo* lives mostly in grassland around rivers and lakes.

The common hippo is the third largest land mammal in the world. It is outweighed only by the largest of the white rhinos and the elephant, the heaviest land animal. The elephant is almost twice as heavy as the common hippo.

In the past, the hippo has been killed for meat, for sport, for its tough hide, and for its ivory. But today, *in preserves only*, the common hippo has increased in number. The hippo has few predators other than lions and leopards that sometimes prey on young hippos. There were many hippos killed by man during the last half of the 19th century, when Africa was being explored and settled by Europeans. And a great many hippos and other animals were killed by poachers during the fighting in Uganda in the 1970s. The hippo is hardy, though. It resists disease and has a long lifespan, living 20 to 40 years in the wild.

Hippos are adapted to an *aquatic* environment—they spend most of their time in the water, only moving onto land at night to graze. By feeding at night, their skin is protected from the sun and the dry air that can cause a serious loss of moisture resulting in *dehydration*.

Because of its bulk, the common hippo may appear awkward on land, but it can move very fast and is considered by many to be the most dangerous animal in Africa. By spending their days in the water and their nights on land, hippos make it difficult for scientists to study them. There is still much to be learned about hippos. The huge hippos, with their big mouths and tiny, twitching ears, have always fascinated humans. As scientists learn more about them, they become even more fascinating.

***I*t's easy to tell** the two types of hippopotamuses apart—because they look so different.

Common hippos are much bigger than their cousins, the pygmy hippos. Common hippos can weigh 3,000 to 7,000 pounds or more. Pygmy hippos weigh only 400 to 600 pounds or about as much as a large hog.

The head and body length of a common hippo can measure 10 to even 15 feet. They stand 5 feet tall at the shoulder. That's twice as tall as a pygmy hippo and three times as long.

Finally, common hippos are as big around as they are long. They have short, heavy legs and huge heads held up by thick necks. Pygmy hippos have smaller heads. They also have longer legs and necks in relation to their bodies.

Pygmy hippos are so secretive, not much is known about them in the wild. They hide in forests and swamps, tunneling through dense growth to reach the water. Pygmies are rare—it seems there have never been very many of them.

■ *Areas where hippos live today*

AFRICA

Thousands of years ago, hippos roamed through Europe, Asia, and Africa. But today, they are only in Africa. Pygmy hippos are found in the forests of West Africa. The huge common hippos live near lakes and rivers in the grasslands of East and Central Africa.

COMMON HIPPOPOTAMUS
Hippopotamus amphibious

ften mistaken for large rocks or floating logs, mmon hippos look like the muddy water where ey spend their days. Waterbirds sometimes perch hippos while fishing or looking for insects.

These pygmy hippos are similar in appearance to a baby common hippo. The characteristics they share are their compact size, small heads, short faces, and proportionately longer neck and legs than the massive adult common hippo.

Common hippos spend most of their time in the water, so all four toes on each hoof are close together to help them swim more easily. Each toe works to support the hippo's tremendous weight out of the water.

Pygmy hippos spend less time in the water than common hippos. Their toes are spread out to help them move more freely on land.

PYGMY HIPPOPOTAMUS
Choeropsis liberiensis

Water plays an important part in the lives of hippopotamuses. They hide in it. They sleep and rest in it during the daytime. And they use it to keep their skin moist. In the hot African sun, a hippo's skin can dry out very quickly. So to protect their skin, hippos either stay in the water or cover themselves with mud.

Hippos lead an *amphibious* life. They move from water to land—and then back to the water. They nap in shallow water or mudholes for most of the day. Then at dusk, they trudge inland to feed.

Hippos prefer slow-moving or still waters. When underwater, they can easily walk along the river bottom. Hippos cannot float, because their heavy muscles weigh them down and cause them to sink. To stay on the water's surface, they have to paddle.

When diving, a hippo presses its ears flat against its head. This keeps out most of the water. When it surfaces, it shakes out the rest by wiggling its ears hard.

Before they dive, hippos take a deep breath and close their nostrils tightly. Adult hippos can stay underwater for as long as five or six minutes. When they come up, they exhale loudly, snorting and hissing as air blasts out of their nostrils.

Hippos are totally hairless except for some patches on the nose, ears, and tail. The hippo's tough hide oozes a sticky pink fluid. This helps keep the animal's skin from drying out in the hot sun and protects the hippo from sunburn.

verything about the common hippo is
eavy. Its head takes up a third of its
dy and can weigh half a ton. And its
in, which is about two inches thick,
n weigh as much as its head!

When swimming, hippos
tuck their short front legs
under their bodies and
kick with their rear legs.

Pygmy hippos
spend more time
on land than in the
water, so their eyes
are on the sides of
their heads—like
those of elephants,
rhinos, and other
land animals.
Their nostrils are
lower, too.

The ears, eyes, and
nostrils of the common
hippo are all on *top* of
its huge head. This lets
the animal hear, see,
and breathe at the
surface while the rest
of its body is safely
hidden underwater.

*A*ll hippos are plant-eating animals, or *herbivores*. But even though hippos spend all day in the water, they rarely feed there. When it's time to eat, they head for the shore.

Every evening at sunset, these hungry giants waddle out of the water. They climb up steep banks and follow well-worn paths to graze in grassy fields. Then, before sunrise, they follow the same paths back to their river, lake, or mudhole.

Hippos eat about 80 to 100 pounds of plants each night. Their favorite food is short grass. Hippos spend only about five or six hours a night grazing. Because the rest of their time is spent lying around in the water or mud, it's safe to say that eating is their main exercise.

For their size, hippos eat very little. Cows, for example, eat almost twice as much as hippos do. Scientists think that hippos eat less because they are experts at saving energy.

In a bad drought, hippos can live for many weeks without food, water, or shade. But they *must* stay in mudholes. To avoid wasting energy, they barely move at all.

When grazing, hippos grab the grass with their lips—which are almost two feet wide! Then they swing their heads to tear off the grass at its roots.

Hippos graze on the same land as buffaloes, elephants, antelopes, and warthogs. But because they eat mainly at night, they usually graze by themselves. Only at dusk are all the animals together.

It can be dangerous to disturb grazing hippos. A male hippo won't hesitate to attack an intruder. And an angry hippo can run much faster than a human!

When grazing, hippos stay close to the water. The farthest they walk to feed is about six miles. Usually they only go half that far.

Hippos are basically gentle animals. They would rather run away than fight. And because of their enormous size and sharp teeth, few animals try to attack them. Mostly hippos fight each other.

Male hippos fight over leadership of a herd. Or they fight over who has control of a water area or mudhole. When two hippos clash, it becomes a contest of weight and strength.

Most hippo fights take place in the water. The opponents move backward side by side in a circle. Then, they swing their massive heads together like sledgehammers.

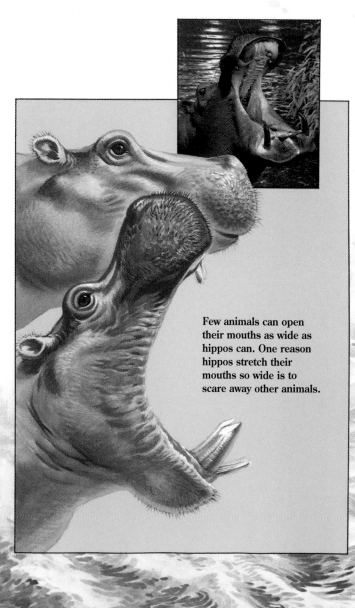

Few animals can open their mouths as wide as hippos can. One reason hippos stretch their mouths so wide is to scare away other animals.

When hippos fight, they
use their razor-sharp
teeth as weapons.

When fighting, hippos use their mouths like buckets to toss water at each other. They also grunt, growl, snort, bellow, honk, and roar as they charge at each other.

The common hippo has two tusk-like canine teeth in its lower jaw. Hippo canines can be up to *20 inches long*, and can weigh more than *4 pounds each*. Like elephant tusks, a hippo's canines keep growing throughout the animal's life.

Hippos often fight for up to two hours, with only short rests. The longest hippo fight on record lasted eight hours!

Young or old, almost all hippos are scarred from fighting. A layer of fat under their thick hide protects their body organs and muscles.

Hippos can do a very special trick. They can turn each ear in a different direction at the same time. As one ear turns forward, the other ear turns backward.

A hippo mother and her young make up the basic hippo family. Hippos gather in herds of 15 to 30 members. But sometimes, as many as 150 hippos crowd together. A male always leads the herd's females and babies.

All hippo mothers protect their young. If anything or anyone gets between a mother and her baby, she gets fighting mad.

Mother hippos often form *nurseries*. They choose the flattest sandy beach near water. Then one or two mothers watch all of the herd's babies—up to 40 young hippos. This frees the other mothers to swim and mate.

Young hippos are often prey for lions and leopards and are sometimes killed by hyenas and crocodiles. So mother hippos must always keep a sharp eye out for trouble. With their powerful jaws, hippo mothers have been known to kill lions and bite crocodiles in half. Young hippos always hide behind their mother for protection

14

Baby common hippos can swim before they can walk. It's a good thing, too, because sometimes they are born underwater and must come up for air right away. Babies can only hold their breath for 20 seconds.

Considering how enormous their parents are, baby common hippos are rather small. They only weigh 100 pounds at birth. An adult hippo can be 80 times bigger than a baby hippo!

A mother hippo rarely gives birth to more than one infant at a time, but she may look after several babies that belong to other mothers. She is very strict about keeping them in a single-file line behind her. If any youngsters wander away or play in line, she nudges or nips at them to get back into position.

Hippos have always fascinated people. Modern hippos in Walt Disney movies wear tutus and dance ever so lightly. A medieval stone hippo on a 13th-century cathedral in Laon, France, has wings. And in ancient Egyptian mythology, the hippo was a goddess that guided departed souls to the afterworld.

Despite their popular appeal, hippos, as well as other animals, have difficulty when their needs conflict with those of humans. Hippos have been hunted and destroyed for many reasons through the centuries. The early Egyptians liked to hunt hippos for their ivory and because they were dangerous animals. Amulets to protect infants from demons were carved from hippo bones.

About 4,000 years ago, there were so many hippos in Egypt that they caused serious crop damage. Egyptian farmers killed them routinely, and by the beginning of the 19th century, all the hippos in that region of Africa had been destroyed.

Hippos were attractions in the arenas of ancient Rome, where people went to see them fight. After the fall of the Roman Empire, hippos weren't seen in Europe again until a few zoos began to exhibit them in the mid 1800s.

People have fashioned false teeth from hippo teeth and whips from tough hippo hide. All the various uses and abuses of the hippo through the centuries have reduced its historic range. Hippos are gone from agricultural areas and regions of spreading human population. Where they do occur, mostly in national parks, they live in such heavy concentrations that they denude the grasslands. This causes other grazing animals to range farther for food, and the hippo, which can't stray far from water, destroys its own feeding grounds.

Concerned about overcrowding, wildlife authorities in Uganda reduced the hippo population in the 1960s. The program seemed successful—the habitat recovered and many species returned. Sadly, war soon broke out in Uganda and large numbers of animals, including hippos, were killed.

Wildlife management programs attempt to achieve a balance between land, animals, and people. This is a delicate undertaking and requires knowledge of the physiology, habits and habitats of the affected animals. It becomes more complicated with changing political situations. For a healthy future, hippos, and other wildlife, require safe places to live, as well as consistent management.

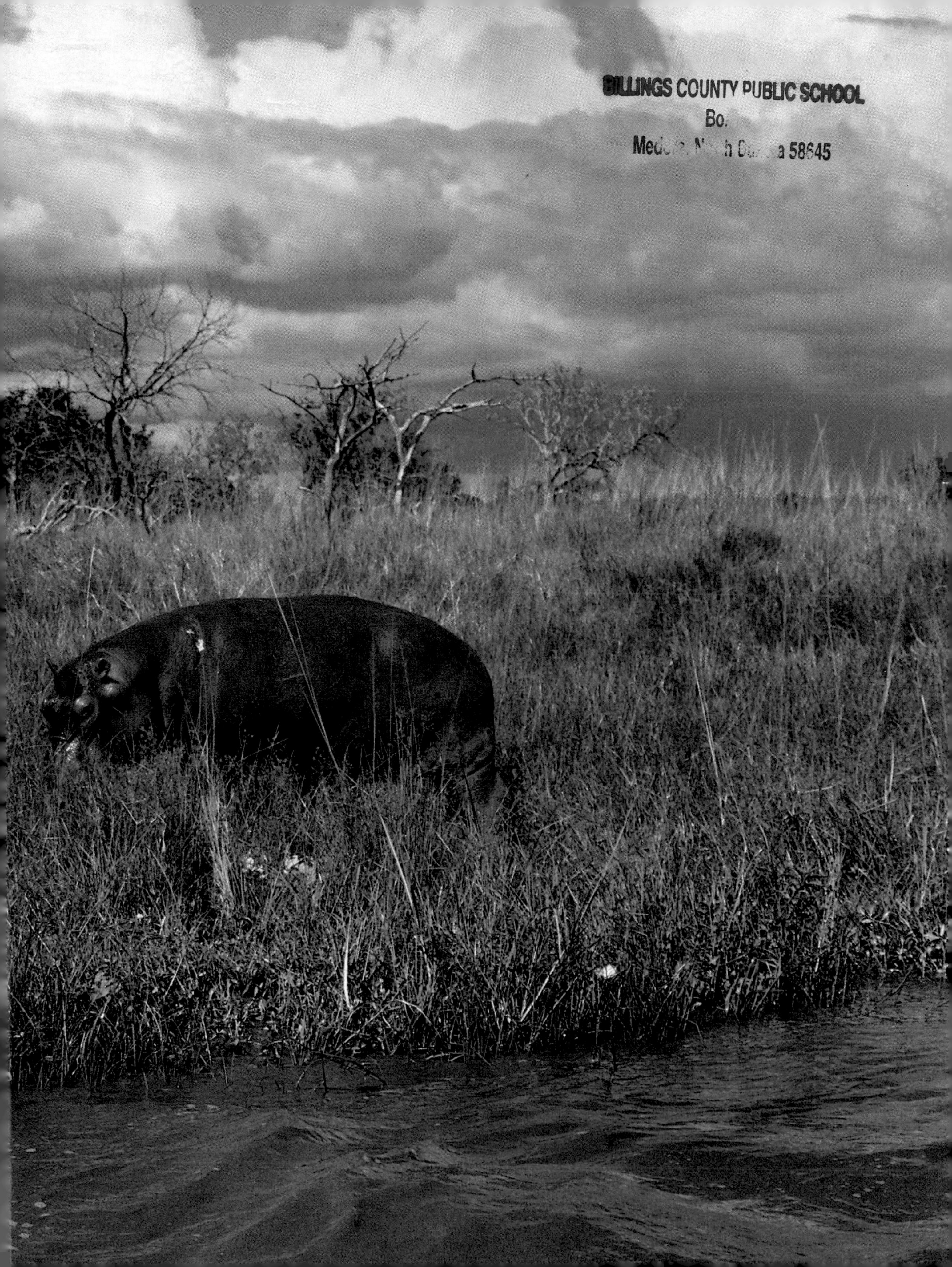

ON THE COVER:
A Common Hippo

Series Created by
John Bonnett Wexo

Written by
Beth Wagner Brust

Scientific Consultant
Phil Robinson, D.V.M.
Member, Hippo Specialist Group
International Union for
Conservation of Nature

Other *ZOOBOOKS* titles:

Alligators & Crocodiles; Animal Babies;
Animal Champions; Animal Champions 2;
Animal Wonders; Apes; Baby Animals;
Baby Animals 2; Bats; Bears; Big Cats;
Birds of Prey; Butterflies; Camels; Cheetahs;
Chimpanzees; City Animals; The Deer Family;
Dinosaurs; Dolphins & Porpoises;
Ducks, Geese, & Swans; Eagles; Elephants;
Endangered Animals; Giraffes; Gorillas;
Hippos; Hummingbirds; Insects; Insects 2;
Kangaroos; Koalas; Lions; Little Cats;
Night Animals; Old World Monkeys;
Orangutans; Ostriches; Owls; Pandas;
Parrots; Penguins; Polar Bears; Rattlesnakes;
Rhinos; Seabirds; Seals & Sea Lions; Sea
Otters; Sharing The World With Animals;
Sharks; Skunks & Their Relatives; Snakes;
Spiders; Tigers; Turtles & Tortoises; Whales;
Wild Dogs; Wild Horses; Wolves; Zebras.

Editorial Production
Marjorie Shaw
Renee C. Burch

Production Artist
Jim Webb

Circulation
John Lee, Manager
Shirley Patino
Laurie Nichols

Controller
Cecil Kincaid, Jr.

Accounting & Administration
Sandra A. Battah
Paula Dennis
Sally Mercer
James F. Blake II

International Licensing Manager
Debra S. Ives

Sales
Julaine Chattaway, Manager
Rejina Freeman
Carmen Rodriguez

Director of Educational Development
Maria Hagedorn

Photographic Credits
Front Cover: Anthony Mercieca (Photo
Researchers); **Inside Front Cover and Page One:**
N. Myers (Bruce Coleman, Inc.); **Page Two:** Simon
Trevor/D.B. (Bruce Coleman, Inc.); **Page Three:**
Norman R. Lightfoot (Bruce Coleman, Ltd.); **Page
Five:** Bruce Coleman (Bruce Coleman, Ltd.); **Page
Seven: Top,** Animals Animals; **Bottom,** Edward R.
Degginger (Bruce Coleman, Inc.); **Pages Eight and
Nine:** Frans Lanting; **Page Ten:** Henry Ausloos (Ani-
mals Animals); **Page Eleven: Top,** Peter Davey
(Bruce Coleman, Inc.); **Center,** Henry Ausloos (Ani-
mals Animals); **Bottom,** E.R. Degginger (Bruce Cole-
man, Inc.); **Pages Twelve and Thirteen:** Charles
Pierson (West Stock); **Page Fifteen: Top,** Marion H.
Levy (Photo Researchers); **Bottom,** Len Rue Jr. (FPG
International); **Page Sixteen and Inside Back
Cover:** E.R. Degginger (Bruce Coleman, Inc.).

Art Credits
Paintings by John Francis.

Printed in the U.S.A.

Wildlife Education, Ltd.®
Poway, California

ISBN 0-937934-54-2

90000
9 780937 934548